# Folkestone
## A Second Selection
### IN OLD PHOTOGRAPHS

THE BANDSTAND

FOLKESTONE

I have had so much on my Shoulders since I've been at Folkestone that I get no Chance to write letters so postcards must do.

# Folkestone
# A Second Selection

## IN OLD PHOTOGRAPHS

Collected by ALAN F. TAYLOR
AND EAMONN D. ROONEY

*Alan Sutton Publishing Limited*
*Phoenix Mill · Far Thrupp*
*Stroud · Gloucestershire*

First published in 1992

Copyright © Alan F. Taylor and
Eamonn D. Rooney 1992

**British Library Cataloguing
in Publication Data**

Taylor, Alan F.
  Folkestone in Old Photographs: Second
  Selection
  I. Title II. Rooney, Eamonn D.
  942.2395

ISBN 0-7509-0132-2

Typeset in 9/10 Sabon.
Typesetting and origination by
Alan Sutton Publishing Limited.
Printed in Great Britain by
The Bath Press, Avon.

DEDICATION: to Anthony Pound, APR Estates, for his 'vision' of the Lanterns.

# Contents

Thomas Cockett was born at Deal around 1809 and came to Folkestone around 1812. The 1861 Census lists his occupation as Sexton and Town Crier; he is shown here in his uniform. The poster he is holding suggests the photograph was taken in 1876.

# Introduction

It is gratifying to be bringing you this second volume of *Folkestone in Old Photographs*. Once we had chosen the photographs for the first selection, the thought occurred to us, 'What would you, the book-buying public, think of our choice?' The success of that book dispelled any doubts that we had got it right. The first selection was so avidly received that it seemed to us nearly everyone in Folkestone had purchased a copy. Some people thanked us personally; others, including one lady now living in Canada, wrote to us to thank us. We in our turn are grateful to you all for your appreciation of our efforts.

In that volume we published a photograph of a John 'Chopper' Anderson, Town Crier of Folkestone (p. 105). It probably came as a surprise to many people to discover that we once had a town crier. However, the post can be traced back to at least 1726 when one John Moon held the office. Others have included Thomas Finn, mentioned in 1758; William Jewel, mentioned in 1809; Thomas Golder, mentioned in 1820; Thomas Cockett (1850s), and J. Surrey in the 1890s. We have included a photograph of Mr Cockett in this volume. The popular image of a town crier is a man in a tricorn hat and knee breeches, which is an eighteenth-century gentleman's walking out dress. The town crier of Folkestone always wore a top hat, frock coat and ordinary trousers.

In this second volume we have chosen to retain some of the most popular sections and add some new ones. We hope that, as a result, these companion volumes will give all those with an interest in Folkestone a comprehensive collection of some of the finest old photographs of the town.

The Stade and Fishmarket section has been retained as it brought so much pleasure to so many. Harbour and Shipping is meant as a tribute to the cross-Channel ferries; to that end we begin the section with a photograph of one of the first fleet and, ignoring the normal age limit for photographs in this series, we finish with a view of MV *Horsa* departing on the final sailing on 31 December 1991, bringing to an end almost 150 years of cross-Channel passenger shipping. The photograph was taken by our good friend Andrew Mullen, for whom this was a very poignant event. The introduction, on 11 April this year, of the Sea-cat service is a welcome restoration of the Channel link.

Streets and Trade contains a fair number of photographs of Rendezvous Street. The inclusion of these will serve as a tribute to Anthony Pound, to whom this volume is dedicated. When next in the Lanterns go and see the restoration job he has wrought on No. 10, then compare it with how it looked when it was Clements shoe shop. This is surely worthy of some sort of award. The Folkestone and District Local History Society mounted an exhibition on Road Transport during the Shepway Festival in 1991 to celebrate seventy-five years of the East Kent Road Car Company. Some of the best photographs are included here.

We hope that the selection of photographs of the Leas will please those who felt that there should have been some in the first volume. We waited until some choice material was available; we think the wait will have been worthwhile. So much of rural Folkestone has disappeared under brick and mortar that we have included some rural views, particularly of the Park Farm area. These are sure to bring back many memories. Private Schools is a subject which would make an absorbing research project for someone. We have included just a few examples of the many such schools once so numerous in the town.

Last but not least is the section titled Folkestone Archaeology. Our knowledge of Folkestone and the surrounding area increases all the time. This year (1992) has seen the discovery of a Bronze Age site at the foot of Caesar's Camp. The photographs of the Jutish burial ground will be new to many people. We have on the East Cliff what is considered by some archaeologists to be some of the finest Roman remains in Britain. Study these photographs, particularly the final one and the aerial view. Most of the foreground in the former has disappeared, i.e. almost to the bath house apse, the curved building clearly seen in the latter. In 1989 a partial excavation took place here which added greatly to our knowledge of the site. Brian Philp of the Kent Archaeological Rescue Unit considers it a very important site and terms the villa 'a small palace'. However, a further partial excavation costing £3,000, planned for 1991, was cancelled because of financial constrictions placed on the Local Authority. Folkestone's Roman heritage is slowly falling over the cliff edge – when will something be done? We must ask this question now. Later generations will, and will wonder why nothing was done.

A.F.T.
E.D.R.
Folkestone, February 1992

# SECTION ONE

# *Stade and Fishmarket*

*Fishing Section. Folkestone.*

This early and unusual view of the Stade dates from just after the turn of the century. On the right is East Street, and in the foreground drift nets are hanging up to dry.

A busy scene on the Stade. Fishermen are cleaning dogfish and mackerel while a small boy looks on. The alleyway in the centre of the picture was known as Jock's Alley.

This early photograph shows the Fishermen's Bethel and North Foreland coffee house. The North Foreland was a public house said to date from 1765. Last licensed in 1879, it was demolished in 1893 and a new Bethel erected.

It is interesting to compare this photograph with the one above. Part of the new Fishermen's Bethel can be seen on the left of the picture.

Luggers at the slipway: the *Invicta*, FE68, the *Emilia Rose*, FE77, and a Rye boat. In the background the Jubilee Inn, Oddfellows Inn and Nickolls sailmakers can be clearly seen.

Fish hawkers' carts and barrows line the Stade outside number one fish shed while an auction is in progress. The railway lines in the right foreground ran from the harbour to the South Eastern and Chatham Railway Company's Marine Workshops.

Sid Harris working in one of the fish sheds repairing a trawl net.

Mrs Lott Waller, fish re-
tailer, at her barrow on the
Stade, *c.* 1935. She is preparing fish for a customer.

Fishermen baiting long lines in fish shed number two in 1936. The building left of the shed
is the new Oddfellows Inn nearing completion.

Looking from shed number three, a cart load of newly tanned drift nets can be seen on the right (under the line of washing). The men by the steps are making a ground rope for a trawl net.

Fishermen unloading fish from their punts at the slipway, c. 1905. Note the old man on the left, who probably 'swallowed the anchor' many years before.

Arthur G. Goddard established his fish merchants business at these premises in Radnor Street in 1899. Mr Goddard (second from the left) and his staff are spitting herrings ready for curing.

Outside the premises of A.G. Goddard and Son, Fish Merchant, 5 the Stade. The business transferred to these premises around 1911 and ceased trading on 21 December 1990. The picture was taken sometime between 1932 and 1935.

The crew of FE15 *Joan of Ark* posing under the stern of the vessel. They are, left to right: John Bull, -?-, Steve Starling, Roland 'Fergy' Noble, Reg 'Knockout' Spicer (skipper), -?-, 'Monjo' Milton, Jim 'Darky' Fagg.

On board FE26 *Flying Fish*, Dave and Dick Spearpoint are hauling long lines, a hard, back-breaking task.

Fishing luggers at anchor, waiting for the tide to come in. The crew of FE38, the boat in the foreground, have 'picked up' their anchor and are rowing into the harbour.

This French fishing boat was brought into Folkestone harbour under arrest having been caught fishing in English waters. The 'B' identifies her home port as Boulogne.

A naval 'steam pinnace' entering Folkestone harbour, *c.* 1905. Her presence would indicate a naval vessel lying off shore.

A lugger from Shoreham, Sussex, moored at the East Head. The paddle-steamers at the South Eastern Railway Company's jetty are possibly the *Myleta* and the *Edward William* which were used for coastal cruises.

The Blessing of the Fisheries is an annual ceremony at the Stade. This picture was taken in 1960. An earlier picture was featured in the first selection of *Folkestone in Old Photographs*.

Harvest Festival at the fishmarket in the 1920s. Among those in the picture are: 'Badger' Allen, Bill Cook, Bill Chapman, William Boorn, 'Bitney' Barton sen., 'Pouty' Fagg, Mrs Skinner, George Skinner, 'Cabby' Hall, Steve 'Redden' Fagg, Wally Walker, and Bill Gale sen.

# Harbour and Shipping

The Cross Channel Ferry Service between Folkestone and Boulogne was inaugurated on 1 August 1843 using three ships: the *William Wallace*, the *Emerald*, and the *City of Boulogne*. This photograph, which dates from around 1858, shows two of the eight vessels built for the service between 1844 and 1847. These were: *Princess Maud, Princess Mary, Queen of the Belgians, Queen of the French, Prince Ernest, Princess Helena, Princess Clementine*, and *Lord Warden*.

Paddle-steamers are rarely seen in the Inner Harbour, as shown in this photograph taken between 1875 and 1880. Behind the tangle of masts on the left can be seen Belle Vue House, now the site of the Shangri-La.

The Outer Harbour, *c.* 1896. The paddle-streamer is the *Duchess of York*, built 1895; the sailing vessel is the *Glencairn*, registered at Folkestone in 1887, owner Thomas Henry Franks. The *Glencairn* sank in 1898.

In this general view of the outer harbour between 1895 and 1899 seven steamers can be seen: five paddle-steamers and two cargo steamers. Note the pleasure craft *Girtie* alongside the South Pier.

The year is 1897, and the building of the extension to the harbour arm has commenced. One of the many steam gantries used in the construction work is in place. The paddle-steamer *Duchess of York* is seen going astern.

The *Girtie*, a sailing pleasure boat owned and operated by Thomas Henry Baker, is seen here leaving Folkestone Harbour. She also operated from the beach near the Victoria Pier.

A large crowd of passengers pose for the camera on board the *Girtie*. The landing stage in the foreground indicates that she is operating from the beach.

Sensational smuggling scene: the noted lugger *Saucy Lass* is being chased by one of HM frigates during a squall in the channel. A tub of brandy can be seen in the water, having been thrown overboard.

Looking towards the parish church from the east before the harbour was built. The *Saucy Lass* is seen running ashore having escaped from the revenue cutter (which is seen going about). This incident took place in about 1804.

The Turbine Steam Ship *Onward*, built in 1905, is discharging her passengers on arrival at Folkestone. The vessel was sold in 1920 and given the name *Mona's Isle*. She operated to and from the Isle of Man until 1947, and was scrapped in 1948.

Captain King and the crew of the *Onward*. In 1899 the London, Chatham and Dover Railway and the South Eastern Railway amalgamated to form the South Eastern and Chatham Railway. *Onward* was the motto of the SER.

The new steel swing bridge being assembled alongside the wooden bridge. The first swing bridge was built in 1847 and replaced by this wooden one in 1893.

A steam gantry stands by to manoeuvre the new steel swing bridge into position in April 1930. The old wooden bridge of 1893 has been dismantled.

A familiar scene at the harbour. The swing bridge is open allowing sailing vessels entry to the inner harbour to unload their cargos.

A similar view to the above. This time the Gas Company's collier *Hove* enters the inner harbour.

A stroll along the South Pier to the 'Horn' lighthouse was a popular pastime, as seen in this *c*. 1914 photograph. The lighthouse probably dates back to 1843.

Before the advent of the roll on–roll off ferries, vehicles were lifted on and off ships by means of a crane. The car in this picture is being unloaded from the Auto Carrier at Folkestone.

The arrival of the Turbine Steam Ship *Invicta* in 1912. *Invicta* was the motto of the London, Chatham and Dover Railway (see p. 26).

The *Isle of Thanet*, built in 1925, was considered the height of cross-Channel luxury for many years. During the Second World War she was used as a hospital ship, after which she was engaged on the Folkestone–Boulogne service until her withdrawal in September 1963.

Folkestone Harbour Station, *c.* 1905. The Great Train Robbery took place here on the evening of 15 May 1855. Gold bullion and American coins to the value of £14,000 were taken.

Folkestone Harbour Station in 1964.

The arrival of the *Maid of Orleans II* at Folkestone. Built in 1949, she worked the Folkestone–Boulogne route until 1972 and from then, until her withdrawal in 1975, she worked the Dover–Calais route.

Cross-Channel Shipping Services from Folkestone ended after nearly 149 years with the departure of the Sealink Stena Line vessel *Horsa* on 31 December 1991. The *Horsa* and her sister ship *Hengist* were built for the route and came into service in 1972. Both vessels were sold in 1992.

# *Streets and Trade*

The Packet Boat Inn, Radnor Street is said to have started in 1811, but probably goes back much earlier under another name. The licence was removed to the East Cliff Pavilion in July 1935 when these buildings were demolished. The fishermen are overhauling herring drift nets.

A delightful study on the Stade, *c*. 1930. Staveley's donkeys line up in front of F. Warman's shipwrights workshop, as a group of children look on. F. Warman became an agent for Petter Oil Engines in 1928 after FE88, the *Elsie*, became the first Folkestone fishing boat to be fitted with a Petter engine in 1927. The Carpenters (formerly the Jubilee Inn) stands on the site of Warman's workshop.

After the demolition of the buildings in the fishmarket area, new retaining walls were built. This photograph, taken 26 November 1935, shows this work in progress at the east end of the Stade.

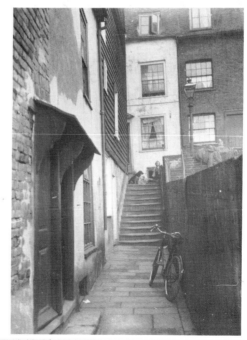

A quaint corner of 'Old Folkestone'. The steps in the picture led up into East Street. See p. 9 for the location of these houses.

A view of Radnor Street, looking west, 1933. The inn sign on the left indicates the Ship Inn. Note the lady in the left foreground perched precariously on a chair, probably cleaning windows.

Radnor Street, looking east in 1928; the junction with North Street can be seen on the left. The gable wall is a profusion of advertising posters including the Pleasure Gardens Theatre and Pier Pavilion.

The right side of Radnor Street from the railway arches. J. Ovenden, Smith and Engineer is still in business today. Further on are St Peter's Men's Club and Whittingstall's general shop.

This rather imposing Georgian entrance gives entry not to a house but a yard – Clout's Alley. The alley led to a group of houses. The photograph was taken on 16 December 1926.

This photograph was taken in Clout's Alley on 25 January 1928 and shows one of the dwelling houses.

A picturesque view of Bate's Alley from North Street. Note the uneven roof on the house in the centre – this house probably dates from the seventeenth century when building commenced in North Street.

A funeral procession in the Tram Road. On the left is the Wonder Tavern, and beyond that the Pavilion Shades and the chimney of Tolputt's timber yard. On the front carriage is John Bridger, livery stable keeper.

A shoeshine boy in Beach Street outside the Wonder Tavern. The building adjoining the Wonder Tavern was the Queens Head Inn.

Jenny Pope's Alley, some time between 1905 and 1912. The sign just
visible on the left is Henry Mills'
fried fish and chip shop, which later
became Hulks.

Beach Street in the 1930s, showing The Olde Arke Dining Rooms (left) and, on the right,
The 'Little Don' barbers shop.

Behind Marine Parade stood two rows of Coastguard Cottages. The gable end of one row can be seen on the right. Some children are posing for the camera. The girl on the left, Lillian Hooker, lived in one of the cottages. The cottages were bombed on 26 August 1940.

Rossi's Corner House Board and Residence, 4 Marine Parade. Mr Rossi was here from 1930 to 1961.

One of Cann's motor coaches outside the True Briton Hotel in 1909, about to leave on a men's outing. The landlord at this period was Mr George M. Carter.

Harbour Street, looking towards Tontine Street. Harbour Street was laid out in 1858. The drinking fountain in the foreground was erected in February 1860 and was removed in around 1922.

The first properties in the vicinity of Bennett's Yard were built just prior to 1720 on land belonging to Ann Trevillion. These houses were pulled down after the Second World War. Bennett Court is named after Bennett's Yard.

A Peace Tea in Dover Street at the junction with Saffron's Place in 1919. The building on the right is the Oddfellow's Inn which started around 1866. The licence was removed to the Hotel Ambassador, the Leas in 1925.

This is thought to be a Coronation street party at Saffron's Place in 1911 to celebrate the accession of King George V.

Dover Street in 1927, just past the junction with Great Fenchurch Street (now St Michael's Street). The shop visible on the left is that of Frederick J. Chadwick, Boot Repairer. On the right is the premises of Walter Wicks, cycle maker.

A group of paper boys pose for the camera outside the newsagents shop of A. Bliss at 42 Dover Street in the 1920s.

Dover Street/Harbour Way in 1958. The corrugated building was formerly used as a chapel to the Convent of the Faithful Virgin. All these buildings were demolished in 1959.

All these properties in Dover Street/Harbour Way were compulsorily purchased by Folkestone Borough Council in 1956. In the background part of the new development can be seen. The furthest building on the right marks the turning into Harvey Street.

Folkestone Carnival, 1922. A decorated milk float of William Howell is seen here in Charlotte Street. Mr Howell is at the horse's head and his daughter Alice is on the float.

An animated scene in Dover Road near the Skew Arches, *c*. 1890. Note the iron toilet in the background; there is still a convenience there today. Some small boys play in the middle of the road while, to the left, a young man carries a lady's bags to the station.

The business premises of Mrs M. Marsh, General Carrier and Fly & Bus Proprietress, at 152 Dover Road. The site today is occupied by Rossendale Court.

No. 43 Dover Road, formerly the vicarage of St Michael and All Angels, later the office of the clerk to the Borough Education Committee. It was demolished to enable Dover Road School playground to be extended in 1924.

Cupola House, 147 Dover Road had many owners over the years. At one time it was occupied by A.E. Glasscock, a mineral water manufacturer. Pembroke Court now occupies the site.

Maud and Albert Marsh with their son Roy stand outside 41 Denmark Street, a fish and chip shop occupied by the family from around 1909 until 1937. This photograph was taken in October 1937. The building was bombed in 1944.

The Alexandra Tavern, 66 Bridge Street, at the junction with Alexandra Street. This off-licence was occupied by the Marsh family from around 1900 to 1944 in which year it was destroyed by a flying bomb.

The Alexandra Dairy was located on the north side of Alexandra Street. This photograph, taken in 1937, shows Arthur Marsh, proprietor from around 1918 to 1938.

An early omnibus picks up a passenger in Black Bull Road. Note the rural situation of the Black Bull Hotel at this time.

Hope Cottage was situated near the Black Bull Hotel. At the time of this picture the cottage was occupied by Albert Burvill, one of Lord Radnor's private policemen.

PHOTO BY     [NEAME, FOLKESTONE.

An advertising card for the Black Bull Hotel, *c*. 1907. The present day Black Bull Hotel was built in 1881 alongside an earlier one of the same name which was then demolished.

This ironmongery and hardware business was started by William Henry Stiles in 1890. Originally known as Fernbank Stores, the name was changed to Crescent Stores after the Second World War. The premises are now occupied by a Chinese Restaurant.

The butchers shop of E.A. Elliott at 26 Black Bull Road at Christmas 1913. Left to right: -?-, -?-, P.H. Elliott, E.A. Elliott, H. Elliott and E.A. Elliott. The business was established in around 1891 and closed in 1960.

This shop was at the junction of Boscombe Road and Ship Street. The lady in the doorway is the wife of Edwin R. Chambers, who ran this confectioners shop from 1908 to 1939. The photograph was taken in 1912.

Flooding in Black Bull Road, October 1939.

Black Bull Road in October 1939. The Imperial Hotel can be seen on the right.

This photograph of 1929 shows public conveniences near the junction with Black Bull Road and Foord Road. In the background can be seen the Public Baths, Silver Spring Mineral Water Works, and the Red Cow Inn.

May Day celebrations in 1909 at Palmerston Street. Among this group are Mr and Mrs Carey, Mrs Ann Lester (left of the maypole, holding Maurice Lester), and Ethel and Annie Lester.

May Day celebrations in 1924 at Palmerston Street. The gentleman on the left is the Revd Cowel, vicar of St John's Church. The gas lamp is on the old meeting house at No. 15, which preceeded St John's Church.

The yard of Mr Fowler, a builder and undertaker, next to the Red Cow Inn, in the aftermath of the flooding of 20 October 1909.

A delightful scene in Foord Road in the early 1900s. Approaching the camera are two boys pulling a hand cart loaded with bushel baskets, while two young girls try to cross the road.

This burial ground stands high above Bradstone Road. In around 1730 this parcel of land was given to the Baptists by one of their number, Mr John Stace, who owned the Bradstone Mill.

Mr A.F. Piggott's General Hardware Stores, 24–28 Foord Road at the junction with New Street. A.F. Piggott was at these premises from around 1892 to 1903. The shop is now Dunn's Heating and Plumbing Supplies.

Mr W.H. Pearson, Coal and Coke Merchants had premises at Grace Hill, Guildhall Street and Foord Road. This picture shows 31 Grace Hill in the 1890s.

Photographs of Peter Street are scarce. This shot, probably taken by an amateur photographer, shows the south side of the street.

In this photograph taken in 1924 the gas lamp marks Vale Yard, Dover Road. The building on the right is now Graham's, Builders Merchants.

The staff of Alfred J. Camburn, Builders, pose outside 1 Dover Road, *c.* 1902. These are now the premises of Hambrook and Johns, Funeral Undertakers.

Nos 14 to 18 Dover Road photographed in 1972 just prior to demolition. The building in the centre of the picture housed the Empress Ballroom which was started in 1947.

Tontine Street, *c.* 1960. Beyond Southern Autos' premises are R.K. Coleman and Son, Coal Merchants, and next to that is the Congregational Sunday school and meeting rooms.

Tontine Street about 1910, showing Freeman Hardy and Willis' shoe shop on the left and Uptons Bazaar on the right. The shoe shop is now Seymore Harrison, Photographic Dealer.

F. Palmer, Hosier and Outfitters at 69 Tontine Street, pictured in 1912. The business was established in 1906 and closed on 20 November 1982.

The tool and cutlery business of Milton and Smith was established at 51 Tontine Street between 1940 and 1947. They moved from these premises to 12 Tontine Street between 1952 and 1954.

Looking south along Mill Bay in February 1928. All the buildings on the right were demolished in 1961; those in the immediate foreground are on the site of the Glass Works.

This photograph of Tontine Street was taken on the same day as the one on p. 64, looking in the opposite direction. Note the three hanging lamps of Messrs Vickery's bootmakers on the extreme right.

Maison Faraoni, Stationer, Bookseller and Bureau de Change, was a popular shop at the bottom of the High Street. The window on the left is well stocked with crested china, including a model of the War Memorial selling at 2s. 9d.

Mr Charles Francis, General Ironmonger was at 69 High Street from 1892 to 1903. These premises were later occupied by Timothy Whites, Chemists and are now the King Tut Restaurant.

Looking up the High Street in 1928. At this time a number of well known shops could be found here, such as International Stores, Home and Colonial, Marks and Spencer, Liptons, and Boots (note their hanging sign on the right).

Another view of the High Street in 1928. The gas lamp marks the opening to the Bayle steps. The shop on the left is May and Sayers, Tailors and Outfitters (Sittingbourne) Ltd.

Looking down the High Street, *c.* 1912. The shop to the right is R. & J. Dick Ltd, Boot and Shoe Dealer, now occupied by Millets, and the shop to the left is Camburns, Butchers, now occupied by Copperfields' Craft, Antique and Collectors' Centre.

This fine drawing depicts the Rendezvous Inn, 1 High Street. The inn was started by Stephen 'Buckle' Hogben in 1866 and the licence expired on 28 December 1912. The property is now the India Restaurant.

This photograph shows the premises of Thomas Taylor's pork butchers shop in Bayle Street. In the doorway are Thomas Fuller Taylor (seated), his grandson Thomas Henry and his children. This business closed in November 1973.

Elizabeth Dorrell, landlady, poses outside the Globe Hotel, The Bayle in 1937. The name was changed to the Guildhall in 1987. Note the upended cannon by the lamp-post. The cannon possibly came from the Battery.

Road resurfacing in Rendezvous Street in 1928. On the right is Fortune's Café and Hambrook and Johns, Undertakers. The canopy on the left marks the entrance to the Savoy Cinema.

These cottages off Rendezvous Street, by the Prince Albert Hotel, were pulled down in 1917.

A congested scene in Rendezvous Street in December 1928. Note the poster advertising 'talkies' at the Savoy, and the Corporation dust-cart outside the Savoy.

John Henry George Brett, who was born at Mersham, started his tailoring business at 24, later 32, Rendezvous Street, c. 1883. The business took the name of L.A. Brett from around 1907 to 1937.

The business of C.J. Saunders, general drapers at 13, 15 and 17 Rendezvous Street, started in 1888. In 1905 the business became Bobby's, who remained at this address till 1931.

E. Whitechurch started his business in 1866 at 7 Rendezvous Street. The business became Whitechurch and Medhurst in 1892 and survived until 1932.

Clements & Son's at 10 Rendezvous Street. The business started in Guildhall Street around 1862, moved here in 1865 and remained till 1898. This frontage was faithfully restored by Anthony Pound, APR Estates.

The Folkestone Gas and Coke Company were at these premises from 1907 to 1937 when they moved to Sandgate Road.

An almost deserted Sandgate Road during the Second World War. Note Sharp's horse-drawn milk float.

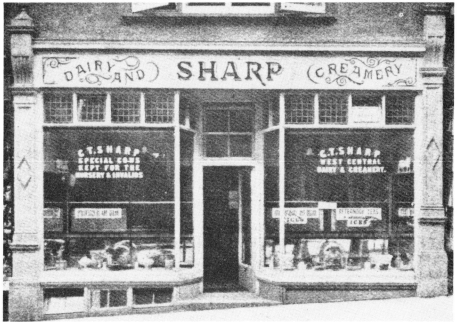

George T. Sharp's West Central Dairy and Creamery was established in 1887. The business moved here in 1896 and remained until around 1959. The premises are now H.G. Samuel, Jewellers.

Sandgate Road, *c.* 1870. On the left is Munckton's Saddlers and Harness Makers, now Clark's Bakery; next door is the National Provincial Bank, now Woolworths.

Bobby and Co's. Department Store, Sandgate Road. Bobby's moved from Rendezvous Street in 1931 to purpose-built premises (the white-fronted building), later extending into the corner premises previously occupied by Lewis and Hyland.

A view of Sandgate Road from Cheriton Place to West Cliff Terrace. The shop on the extreme left is Hudson Brothers, Grocers and Provision Merchants, who were in business at these premises from 1912 to 1969.

The Scottish Tea Rooms, 77 Sandgate Road (1906–1908) is now occupied by Sketchleys, Dry Cleaners. It is now 89 Sandgate Road.

Sandgate Road, c 1910. Note that all the buildings this side of Cheriton Place are residential. The man on the bicycle marks the access to Sainsburys.

The grocery shop at 16 Bouverie Road West of William Hollis, who started trading at these premises in 1902 and remained here until 1916. This photograph was taken around 1910.

The West Cliff Pharmacy of Messrs Hall and King, 24 Bouverie Road West, which commenced business around 1893. These premises survive to this day with much the same appearance, including the large lamp.

Arthur Stace & Sons, 22 Bouverie Road West (next to Hall and King). The stationery business of Stace & Sons started in 1926 and ran until sometime between 1940 and 1947. The lady on the left is Mrs Radcliffe and the photograph was taken October 1932. The shop is still a stationers and newsagents.

One of Folkestone's oldest established businesses. In around 1906 G. & A. Clark succeeded William Buzan as nurserymen in Cheriton Road. The business was established in 1863 primarily as nursery gardens. Rose Cottage in Cheriton Road is thought to have been built in connection with the gardens.

Bill Chadwick, a delivery boy for G. & A. Clark. These delivery boys and their bicycles were once a regular sight around the town.

Howard and Co., high class family grocers, were at 100 Cheriton Road, at the junction with Brockman Road, from 1907 to 1970.

An Edwardian view of Coolinge Road. Note the various tradesmen going about their business, including a milkman (left background) and, in the foreground, a fish hawker.

William George Howell, Dairyman of 18 Radnor Bridge Road, seen here in Bouverie Square. Note the gardens in the background which were swept away in 1955 to create the bus station.

The north-west side of Bouverie Square, looking towards No. 23 (the site of which is now occupied by the multi-storey car park), in April 1905. Note the paper delivery boy on the right.

These buildings, which stood on the north-east side of Bouverie Square, were pulled down in 1976 and replaced by a supermarket which is now an indoor market. Martin Walters, on the right, is now part of the Job Centre.

The milk delivery hand cart of George T. Sharp and Sons pictured outside 14 Bouverie Square. Note the large container complete with tap, from which the milk measures were filled – a practice which would not be allowed today.

Looking up Bouverie Road East in the 1960s. All these properties were demolished in 1972 to facilitate the construction of the Northern Distributor Road.

Christ Church School, at the junction of Bouverie Road East with Cheriton Road, opened in 1852 and was known as the 'Gun School'. It was replaced in 1955 by a new school in Brockman Road.

Cheriton Road at its junction with Guildhall Street, showing the Shakespeare Hotel on the right. All the buildings on the right as far as the eye can see were demolished in 1972.

A very interesting photograph in Cheriton Road. The tall chimney belongs to the Gun Brewery, established in 1846. Compare this photograph with the one on p. 90.

The junction of Bouverie Road East with Cheriton Road, looking towards Guildhall Street, *c.* 1967. The buildings on the right have been demolished and the site is used as a car park. A market is held there every Thursday.

George Strood, Baker and Pastrycook, started in business in 1874 at 30 High Street. After a short time in Dover Road he moved to these premises at 60 Guildhall Street in 1887 where he remained till 1906.

The junction of Guildhall Street with Shellons Street and Cheriton Road, *c.* 1905. At the foot of the lamp-post, next to the Shakespeare Hotel, is an upturned Tudor gun thought to have come from the Bayle Battery. It was from this that the Gun School and Gun Tavern and hence Gun Corner took their names.

H.G. Birch, Wine and Brandy Importer of 5 Guildhall Street, established 1890, was taken over by Prentis and Sons in 1924. It continued as an off-licence until the late 1980s.

Shellons Street in May 1972. Demolition on this side of the street has commenced prior to construction of the Northern Distributor Road.

The Northern Distributor Road is now in place and a car park constructed on the centre reservation. All that remains of the houses in the picture are the two with arched doorways on the right.

A bird's eye view of Guildhall Street, c. 1910. Note the early motor vehicle in the background and Pickfords removal van in the foreground. The Queens Hotel is very prominent on the left.

An unusual photograph taken in Guildhall Street looking towards the Town Hall. The shop in the immediate foreground is Harvey Williams. Note that No. 12 was still a private residence when this picture was taken.

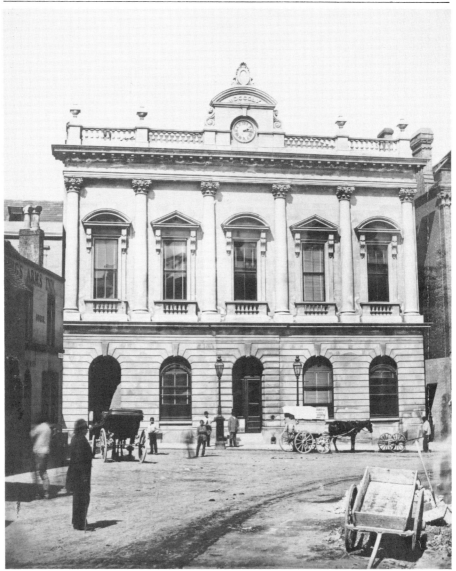

The properties on the corner of Sandgate Road and Church Street had been demolished by the summer of 1862. The dark line marks the original building line, the opportunity having been taken to widen the road. Note that the Town Hall is as originally constructed, without a porch.

# Transport and Outings

A coaching revival took place in the Edwardian era. Many a coach-and-four operated at Folkestone, including the 'Empress', the 'Rover' and the 'Active'; the latter is thought to be the coach picture here outside the Metropole Hotel, *c.* 1910. Note the rather large telescope at the hotel entrance.

The 'Rover' preparing to set off for Folkestone Races from outside the East Kent Arms, c. 1913. The coach was one of many owned by Frank Funnel, landlord of the East Kent. The entrance to the livery stables can be seen in the background.

The carriage seen here at the north side of the Bouverie Square belonged to Mr John Bridger, livery stable keeper of Christ Church Road, and was hired for the wedding of Miss Sydney Brooke and Captain Leslie Claude Dormen on 25 November 1911.

William Thomas Anderson, firewood merchant of 1a Linden Crescent, pictured here with his horse Hettie. Mr Anderson was in business from 1931 to 1940–7.

The milk float of F. Kennett, Metropole Dairy, Coolinge Lane is pictured here in Foord Road. The dairy was established in 1892 and finished trading in 1917.

Clarence Street in 1917. An early steam lorry has skidded on the ice. The vehicle belonged to G.W. Chitty, flour millers of Dover.

A coach outing operated by the London and South Coast Motor Services Limited preparing to set off from the Harbour Hotel, 24 Harbour Street, *c.* 1905.

This charabanc D3335, operated by E.V. Wills, was built by Maltby's of Sandgate in 1907. It is seen here outside 5 Rendezvous Street just before the First World War. The driver is thought to be Mr Piddock.

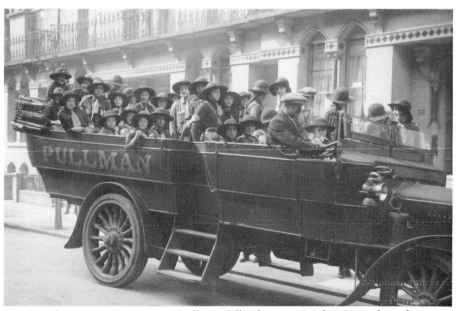

A girl guides' outing to a County Rally at Gillingham on 3 July 1926, where they were inspected by Princess Mary. Nine charabancs went from Folkestone, departing from Alexandra Gardens.

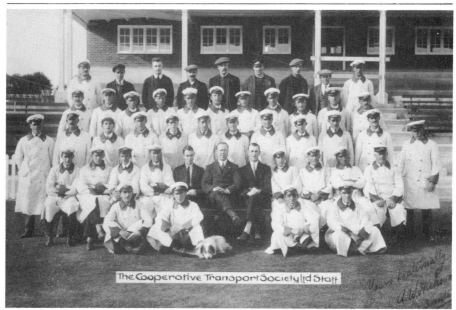

The Folkestone Co-Operative Transport employees pictured at Folkestone Cricket Ground in 1926.

Christ Church Choir outing pictured at 20 Brockman Road in 1925. The vehicle KN9502 is a 40 hp Dennis 28-seater acquired by Wills in July 1920.

A ladies-only outing preparing to leave from under the railway arch leading to Radnor Street. The picture is thought to have been taken just after the First World War.

Christ Church Choir outing pictured at 2 Clifton Road.

Another Christ Church Choir outing, this time pictured at 51 Brockman Road.

Three charabancs of London and South Coast Motor Services at Bayle Parade. The double door on the left is the store belonging to Plummer Roddis, Drapers and Complete House Furnishers.

The office of the London and South Coast Motor Services Ltd, at 6 Sandgate Road, *c.* 1915. J. Cann, the proprietor, stands in the doorway. Note the day trip to Eastbourne, 12s., and the 'Health Trips'.

An East Kent Tilling Stevens charabanc parked outside the Black Bull Hotel, *c.* 1920. The occasion is an outing of the Folkestone Electricity Company's staff.

This photograph, taken at Cherry Garden Avenue in July 1929, shows some of a total of sixty-one 'cars' employed by the East Kent Road Car Company in the execution of a private hire contract.

A Guy Utility, BJG417 registered in 1945, is seen parked on the south side of Bouverie Square, *c*. 1955. This vehicle spent most of its working life at Folkestone.

Pictured here in Bouverie Square is a Leyland PD1 CJG984. This vehicle was registered in 1948 and spent most of its working life at Folkestone. Note the construction of the East Kent offices.

A Guy Arab, FFN366 registered in 1951, came to Folkestone in 1959. The destination board reads Shorncliffe Camp; this was service 99.

This Guy Arab, GFN911, was registered in 1953 and operated from Canterbury depot. It is parked on the west side of Bouverie Square.

An open-top bus on Dover Hill in 1963. The passengers are possibly watching the *Maid of Orleans* manoeuvring to go astern into the harbour.

William Frost and Sons, Private Hire Luxury Coaches, were in business until the mid-1950s. Their office was at 141 Sandgate Road, and is now occupied by a video rental company.

Radiotax were in business at Bouverie Square from around 1952 to around 1960, and were succeeded by United Taxis. The rural scenery in the background is now, alas, covered by the Channel Tunnel Terminal complex.

Folkestone Taxi Company is thought to have been established immediately after the Second World War at 113 Sandgate Road, from which address they still operate today.

This delivery van, belonging to James Emberson, Baker and Confectioner of 5 Dover Street/Harbour Way, is a Model 'T' Ford registered in London in June 1923. Embersons were in business from around 1898 until 1943.

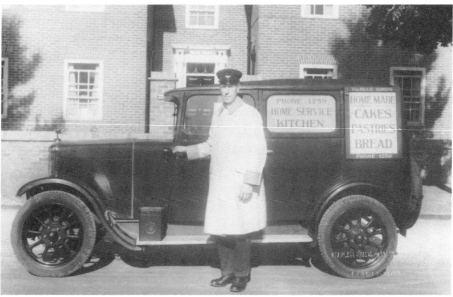

Louise Home Service Kitchen, 1a and 1b Cheriton Place. This photograph, taken on 22 August 1930, shows Mr Mullett with his delivery van.

This Chrysler was driven by Mr G.S. Bouwar and Mr E. Millin from the Cape to London via Cairo in 1928. The vehicle, seen here parked outside Auto Pilots Garage, set a record for the journey.

The winner of the French Grand Prix outside Auto Pilots Garage in 1926.

A traction engine, possibly built by Clayton and Shuttleworth and owned by C.J. Nickolls, pulls two containers belonging to Davis and Davis. This photograph was taken around 1915.

A later Davis and Davis (formerly Adolphus Davis) vehicle seen here taking part in a carnival procession.

An early fleet belonging to Thompson and Son, Removal Contractors, possibly photo-graphed at Cherry Garden Avenue. The business was established just after the First World War and ceased trading in the mid-1950s.

A later Thompsons' vehicle seen here at the bottom of the Road of Remembrance in 1933.

# *Seafront*

An aerial view of Folkestone seafront, *c.* 1948, showing the burnt out remnants of the Victoria Pier. The pier pavilion burnt out on Whit Monday 1945 and was finally demolished in 1954. Note that the Leas, Marine Gardens and foreshore are unaffected by modern development.

The Old Clockhouse Building being demolished around 1899 to make way for an extension to the Pavilion Hotel. The Clockhouse was built in 1843 as residence for the harbour master and offices for the South Eastern Railway Company. The building had elements of Venetian architecture.

Crazy golf at the Marine Gardens in the 1930s. A crowd looks on as three ladies play the next hole.

A busy scene on the beach, *c.* 1905. Both of Fagg's patented bathing wagons are at the water's edge, and a number of small bathing wagons are also in use.

Pleasure boats plying for hire. On the *Skylark II*, in the foreground, the boatmen raise their arms indicating that there are a few seats remaining. Their cry would have been, 'Any more for this trip, we're just-a-leaving.'

The motor vessel *Josephine* ready to discharge her passengers after returning from a trip. This is a trade which has completely died out.

Dick Baker, born in 1847, was eighty-six years of age when this photograph was taken. It is said that his beach hut had been the deckhouse of the sailing ship *Baron Holberg* which was driven ashore in a gale on 25 September 1896. The deckhouse made of teak is now in the garden of a house in Cornwallis Avenue.

Tom Saunders, beach inspector for Folkestone Corporation in the 1930s. Among his duties was the safety of the bathers, raising the red flag when it was dangerous to bathe, or red cone to prohibit bathing. He was also responsible for regulating the boatmen. The office of beach inspector was created in June 1887.

When not in use, the pleasure boats' landing stages made good diving platforms. Note the young lady at extreme right about to photograph her two friends.

These kiosks stood on the seaward side of the Marine Gardens. The one in the foreground belongs to John Osmond and the sign proclaims, 'Get your bargains here and save money.'

'The Chocolate King' kiosk can be seen in the picture above, alongside John Osmond's kiosk.

Jack 'the Racker' Penfold, a local fisherman photographed outside the bathing cabins which were situated near the Marine Gardens.

Mr E.D. Winter was typical of the many boatmen who operated from the beach. He supported himself by hiring out deck-chairs and rowing boats. For the location of Mr Winter's hut see p. 125.

A very clear photograph of the Sea Bathing Establishment. Constructed in 1868, it opened in July 1869. In the background are Priory Gardens and the Vicarage.

The Bathing Establishment later had an extension added, as seen in this view, to accommodate a larger swimming pool which was later covered over to make a dance floor. The name was changed to the Marina after the Second World War. The Marina closed in 1958 and was demolished in 1966.

An aerial view of the seafront, showing the Leas Lift, the Marina, the Red Roof Chalet and, in the foreground, the Open Air Swimming Pool. Apart from the lift, none of these amenities exist today.

The Bathing Pool was opened in 1936 which may have been when this photograph was taken. Note the Victoria Pier in the background, with a notice announcing 'Undress Wear Parade 9–10' – a beauty competition?!

The young ladies of Folkestone Swimming Club. The girl at the centre of the picture, Pearl Martin, was their leading prize winner. In the background is the Rowing Club headquarters.

Pearl Martin photographed in 1920 during Folkestone Regatta wearing the first 'jazz' bathing costume seen in the town. With her is Sir Philip Sassoon.

Folkestone Rowing Club Junior and Senior Four were South Coast Champions in 1904. They are, left to right: R. Ward (stroke), G. Finn, E. Heron (bow), S. Pope. Sitting is B. Comer (cox). They are posing outside the Rowing Club headquarters, Lower Sandgate Road.

A cluster of kiosks near the Victoria Pier, *c.* 1928, including the Co-Operbancs booking office, H.M. Drake, Newsagent and Tobacconist, and Rossi's Ice-cream.

The foreshore near the Bathing Establishment, *c.* 1900. A lady and young girl relax by the perambulator in the foreground. In the background is the lifeboat house, and to the right is a camera obscura, in front of which is Mr Winter's hut.

Peep Lower Sandgate Road Folkestone.

A rather unusual view of the Victoria Pier framed by the pine trees of the Lower Sandgate Road. The picture illustrates the structure of the pier in very fine detail.

Thompson's Patent Gravity Switchback Co. Ltd constructed this railway in 1888. It commenced operating on Friday 17 August 1888 shortly after midday and continued running free of charge until 1 o'clock.

The Beach and Marine Promenade from the Victoria Pier in the 1930s. The Marine Promenade was built in 1910. In the foreground are just two of the many rowing boats which were available for hire.

Mr Thomas Sinclair outside his ticket office which was known as 'Uncle Tom's Cabin'. He took over the switchback in 1909 and is thought to have operated it until 1915. In 1925 it was dismantled and the materials sold to an Ashford timber merchant for £500. Tom Sinclair died on 8 February 1930.

The beach and promenade are crowded with people in this 1930s photograph. The building in the centre housed changing rooms for bathers. Note the deck-chair attendant issuing tickets.

There were many places along the seafront at which to take refreshments. This one, the Zig-Zag Café, was situated about midway between the Mermaid Café and Victoria Pier.

The type of vessel seen here is a spritsail barge. Most of these vessels were wooden-hulled, but because of its steel hull this one was known as an 'Iron-Pot'. The *Astrild* is shown here in 1907 stranded on Mill Point but she was refloated and survived into the 1950s.

## SECTION SIX

# *The Leas*

Armistice Day, 11 November 1929. The mayor, Councillor Albert Castle, is placing a wreath at the War Memorial on the Leas.

The east end of the Leas by Albion Villas. The gun on the right is of Tudor origin and is believed to have come from the Bayle Battery. On the left is the ornamental fountain unveiled in February 1898 in memory of Sydney Cooper Weston (1842–93). It now stands on the East Cliff.

The Leas in the early years of the century, just after the building of the Leas Pavilion which opened in 1902 and can be seen on the right.

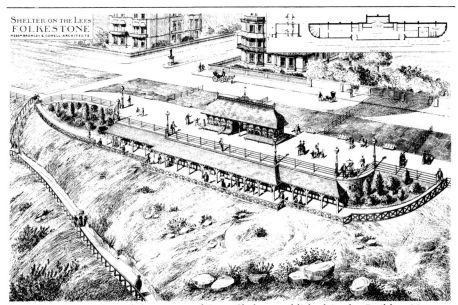

An artist's impression of the proposed Leas Shelter, published in the *Builders News* on 20 April 1888. The design was by Messrs Bromley and Cowell, Architects.

The Leas Shelter opened in 1894, six years after the above plan was published. Note that the ornamental shelter on the Leas was not included.

The Central Hall of the Leas Shelter was 62 ft by 31 ft and was used for daily orchestral concerts in the spring, autumn and winter. In 1927 it was enlarged and became the Leas Cliff Hall.

A gentleman in a top hat gazes at the statue of William Harvey (1578–1657). The statue by Albert Joy was unveiled in 1881 and the railings were added in 1882.

A late afternoon on the Leas in the 1880s. People have gathered to listen to the band. While most people are oblivious of the photographer, he has caught the attention of the boy on the left.

76   FOLKESTONE. — Earls Avenue. — LL.

Earls Avenue, *c.* 1910. The traffic in the picture is horse-drawn except for the early motor car on the right. The Burlington Hotel can be seen on the left.

Lord Radnor's policeman (wearing medals) can be seen on his beat on the Leas in 1905. The distinctive canopied deck-chairs around the bandstand were introduced to the Leas in 1881.

In this photograph, taken in the late 1890s, all attention is focused on the policeman (extreme left) who is escorting an 'undesirable' off the Leas.

First World War Rest Camp Number 3, Clifton Crescent, the Leas. This rest camp included a YMCA building which can be seen on the extreme left.

SOUTH WEST VIEW (FROM LEAS)
Nº3 REST CAMP FOLKESTONE. (Nº 18)

Another view of Rest Camp Number 3, looking east. These rest camps received troops preparing to cross the Channel and those returning from the battle front.

A rare Victorian view at the west end of the Leas. The building on the right is now the Salisbury Hotel and Clifton Crescent is seen in the distance.

It is interesting to compare this photograph of Clifton Crescent taken after the First World War with that on p. 137. There are a number of cars, including an Austin Seven, parked in the background.

The wheelhouse of the Metropole Lift on a breezy day in the 1920s. Two children run away while a group of people wait to take a ride on the lift.

A good close-up view of one of the cars on the Metropole Lift which opened in 1904. Mr Collins the liftman poses for the camera.

The Metropole bandstand in the 1920s. A large crowd has gathered to listen to the band.

West Leas looking east in 1908. Note the rather elegant lady with her parasol and, to her right, the perambulator with its lace-edged sun shade. A good example of a bath-chair is parked by the lamp-post.

# Rural Folkestone

Although the main feature of this 1921 photograph is transport, we have used it as the opening of this section because of the clear view of Walton Manor Farm it provides. This was one of the oldest farms in the area, mentioned in the Domesday Book (1086) and recorded in 1095 as belonging to the Manor of Folkestone. The farm buildings were cleared away in the mid-1960s and Walton Manor Close was built on the site. The fleet of charabancs in the foreground were part of a new fleet acquired by the newly formed (1916) East Kent Road Car Company.

The *Folkestone Herald* reported on 23 May 1903 that, 'Today the Royal East Kent Imperial Yeomanry assemble at Folkestone for their annual training.' This photograph shows the Yeomanry encamped in the field at the corner of Cheriton Road and Cherry Garden Avenue.

A rural view of Cherry Garden Avenue in 1935, showing Broadmead Manor House. The farmhouse was built in 1711.

Further down Cherry Garden Avenue, approaching the premises of the Folkestone and District Water Company, whose chimney can be seen in the background.

A peaceful scene at Park Farm. Some of the haystacks belonging to Park Farm can be seen on the left and, in the distance, the chimneys of Park Farm Brick Works. Today this is an industrial estate.

Nestling among the trees in about 1910 is Park Farm Cottage, and to the left are the cow sheds.

Another view of Park Farm, this time from the other side of the path. The row of trees in the background marks the line of what is now Churchill Avenue.

The field pictured here is now the site of Holywell Avenue. It is hard nowadays to imagine the harvest being gathered there as in this photograph taken in 1928.

Ploughing in the fields between Caesar's Camp and Sugarloaf Hill in 1941.

The tree-lined avenue seen here was laid out just before the First World War. Although it had been laid out, it was not completed until 1970, and was named Churchill Avenue.

This charming view, with cows grazing in the fields, is now a residential area. Scenes like this will never be seen so close to the town again.

Looking from Sugarloaf Hill across open countryside toward Park Farm and the town in 1913. In the distance is the viaduct and the roof tops of Mead Road and Russell Road.

Wingate Hill Cottage, better known as 'Granny May's', is thought to have been a toll house. It was later the residence of the quarry keeper.

Another view of Granny May's, this time looking from Sugarloaf Hill. This picture was taken in 1913 and shows a group of ladies and children out for a walk. The cottage was run by Morris Roach as a tea rooms until 1962 and was demolished in 1963.

# SECTION EIGHT

# *Private Schools*

There was a profusion of private schools in the town during the Victorian and Edwardian eras. Abbotsford School for Boys was started at Castle Hill Avenue in 1900 by John Abbott and later relocated to 40 Shorn Cliffe Road some views of which are shown on this ornately decorated postcard.

The Grange, Shorncliffe Road was a private school for young gentlemen opened by the Revd A. Hussey between 1883 and 1885. The school was closed around 1935 but reopened in 1937 as the Technical Institute and Junior Commercial School.

This view of the Grange shows the playground and rear view of the school. The school is now South Kent College.

St Nicholas's School was in Sandgate Road on the corner of Trinity Gardens. It was a private school for young ladies and was opened between 1885 and 1887 as the Girls' Collegiate School by a Mrs Badham. A Miss Sophia Purton took over the school around 1893.

The school was renamed St Nicholas's in 1905 and closed in 1924. This illustration shows the senior girls' study.

Kent College, 6 Grimston Avenue (corner of Bouverie Road West) was a school for middle-class Wesleyan Methodist girls. It was opened in 1886 by a Miss Chudleigh.

Some of the girls enjoy a game on the hockey field at Kent College. The school closed between 1940 and 1947 and is now a complex of flats.

Praetoria House School for Young Gentlemen started at 1 Grimston Avenue between 1885 and 1887. It took its name from A.P. Praetorious who started the school. The school moved to these premises in Coolinge Lane in 1904.

This photograph shows the classroom of Form II at Coolinge Lane. After Praetoria House School had moved out, 1 Grimston Gardens became Mayfield House School for Young Ladies. Praetoria House is now the Girls' Grammar School.

Gloster House School of Household Management, 5 Shorncliffe Road. Under the principal Miss Julian, the school was here from 1912 to 1916. It is now the police station.

# *Folkestone Archaeology*

## ANGLO-SAXON REMAINS
## DOVER HILL, FOLKESTONE

### 1907.

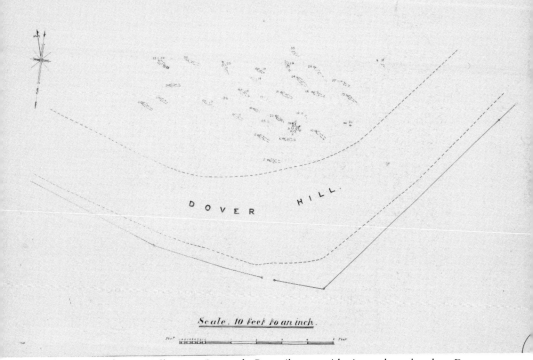

Scale. 10 feet to an inch.

In the winter of 1907 Folkestone Borough Council were widening a sharp bend on Dover Hill. In doing this a number of skeletons were disturbed and it soon became clear this was a Saxon burial ground. As with most of the others found in Kent, a southern slope had been chosen for the site. In this excavation and a further excavation in 1910 a total of forty graves were found.

A view looking south across the burial ground towards the town.

This close-up of part of the site shows a number of the burials in greater detail.

When the burial ground was discovered, one of the skeletons was removed to the museum at Grace Hill. At that time it was the only complete Saxon skeleton in any museum in the world.

Some of the arms and ornaments found at the burial ground. These, and the complete skeleton, are now in the Folkestone Museum at Grace Hill.

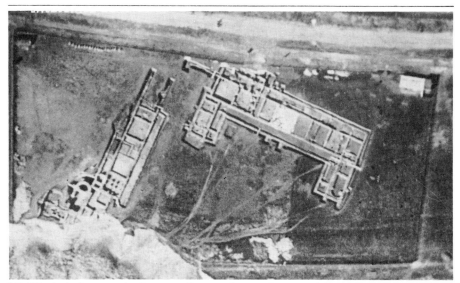

S.E. Wimbolt discovered a Roman villa complex on the East Cliff in 1924. This aerial view shows its proximity to Wear Bay Road. The main villa adjacent to the road is known as block 'A' and that at right angles as block 'B'.

The remains of the tessellated floor which was found in block 'A'.

The hypocaust of the bath house apse can be seen by the cliff edge in the aerial photograph on the previous page. This area was the subject of a partial re-excavation in 1989.

Looking towards Wear Bay Road with the bath apse in the foreground. Much of the foreground in this picture has now slipped down the cliff. The site has been grassed over and is used as a car park.

# *Acknowledgements*

This publication has been compiled solely from the collections of Alan Taylor and Eamonn Rooney and the late C.P. Davies. Alan and Eamonn are indebted to those people who over the years have given items of have allowed photographs to be copied, thus helping to build their collections.

We would like to offer sincere thanks to the following people:

Mr K. Bridger • Miss M. Paterson • Mrs Rene-Martin • Mr J. Slade
Mr Collins • Mr W.S. Warman • Mr J. Brickell • Mr F. Foot
Mr C. Thompson • Mr M. Fagg • Mr G. Ball (Ball Signs) • Mr J. Hall
Mr J. McLaren • Mr E. Warman • Mrs D. Heaver • Mr K. Smith
Mrs Williams • Mr W. Lester • Mr R. Bliss • Mr D. McDine • Mr G. Elliott
Mr Burville • Mr R. Humphreys • Mrs Titley • Miss M. Sidey • Mr B. Hart
• Mrs I. Brady • Mr R.J. Palmer • Mr L. Jeggo • Mrs P. Martin.

Sincere thanks are also due to the staff of Guildhall Camera Centre for all their help over the years.